A Note From Rick Renner

I am on a personal quest to see a "revival of the Bible" so people can establish their lives on a firm foundation that will stand strong and endure the test as end-time storm winds begin to intensify.

In order to experience a revival of the Bible in your personal life, it is important to take time each day to read, receive, and apply its truths to your life. James tells us that if we will continue in the perfect law of liberty — refusing to be forgetful hearers, but determined to be doers — we will be blessed in our ways. As you watch or listen to the programs in this series and work through this corresponding study guide, I trust you will search the Scriptures and allow the Holy Spirit to help you hear something new from God's Word that applies specifically to your life. I encourage you to be a doer of the Word He reveals to you. Whatever the cost, I assure you — it will be worth it.

> Thy words were found, and I did eat them;
> and thy word was unto me the joy and rejoicing of mine heart:
> for I am called by thy name, O Lord God of hosts.
> — Jeremiah 15:16

Your brother and friend in Jesus Christ,

Rick Renner

Beware of Deceptive Times

Published by Rick Renner Ministries
www.renner.org

ISBN 13: 978-1-6675-0354-7

eBook ISBN 13: 978-1-6675-0355-4

How To Use This Study Guide

This one-part study guide corresponds to *"Beware of Deceptive Times"* *With Rick Renner* (Renner TV). It covers topics that are addressed during the program series, with questions and references supplied to draw you deeper into your own private study of the Scriptures on this subject.

To derive the most benefit from this study guide, consider the following:

First, watch or listen to the programs prior to working through this study guide. (Programs can also be viewed at **renner.org** by clicking on the Media/Archives links or on our Renner Ministries YouTube channel.)

Second, take the time to look up the scriptures included in this lesson. Prayerfully consider their application to your own life.

Third, use a journal or notebook to make note of your answers to the Study Questions and Practical Application challenges.

Fourth, invest specific time in prayer and in the Word of God to consult with the Holy Spirit. Write down the scriptures or insights He reveals to you.

Finally, take action! Whatever the Lord tells you to do according to His Word, do it.

For added insights on this subject, it is recommended that you obtain Rick Renner's book *How To Keep Your Head on Straight in a World Gone Crazy.* You may also select from Rick's other available resources by placing your order at **renner.org** or by calling 1-800-742-5593.

TITLE
Beware of Deceptive Times

SYNOPSIS

When Jesus was asked about the sign of His coming and the end of the world, the first thing He said was, "…Take heed that no man *deceive* you" (Matthew 24:4). Webster's original 1828 dictionary defines the word "deceive" as *to mislead the mind; to cause to err; to cause to believe what is false, or disbelieve what is true.*[1] Moreover, this definition indicates that a person who is "deceived" is one who has been *deluded, cheated,* and *robbed.* More than four times in His Olivet discourse, Jesus warned us that widespread deception will abound in the last days (*see* Matthew 24). Therefore, it is imperative that we understand what we're up against and learn to embrace the only effective remedy against deception — the truth of God's Word.

The emphasis of this lesson:

We're living in the perilous period prophesied by Jesus and Paul — a time when deception will run rampant, and people will depart from the faith. Many are questioning their moral beliefs and slowly distancing themselves from the biblical standards they once embraced. A domino effect of degradation has been set in motion. Rebellion, anarchy, and lawlessness have reached unprecedented levels, and we've become a reprobate generation. It is the Holy Spirit in the Church that is restraining evil from engulfing humanity, and it is God's Word in our hearts and minds that will empower us to live in victory in these last days.

The Disciples Asked Jesus About the End Times

There is a very interesting conversation between Jesus and His disciples recorded in three of the four gospels. Matthew wrote, "And Jesus went out, and departed from the temple: and his disciples came to him for to shew him the buildings of the temple" (Matthew 24:1). This temple was the one built by Herod the Great and took more than 40 years to construct, and although it was not as magnificent as the original temple built by King

Solomon, it was splendid nevertheless with each side measuring "a stadium" according to the historian Josephus.[2]

The Bible goes on to say, "And Jesus said unto them, See ye not all these things? verily I say unto you, There shall not be left here one stone upon another, that shall not be thrown down" (Matthew 24:2). Immediately after these words left Jesus' lips, the disciples began to internally question what He meant. *How can this be?* they thought. *How in the world are these massive stones going to be thrown down and scattered?*

Once the disciples were away from the multitudes, they looked for an opportunity to talk with Jesus. The Bible says, "And as he sat upon the mount of Olives, the disciples came unto him privately, saying, Tell us, when shall these things be? and what shall be the sign of thy coming, and of the end of the world?" (Matthew 24:3) In this verse, there are five very important words that we need to understand. They are: "when," "what," "sign," "end," and "world."

Five Key Words in the Disciple's Question

'WHEN shall these things be?' This is the first question the disciples asked Jesus. The word "when" is the Greek word *pote*, and it describes *specific information* or *a concrete answer*. Essentially, the disciples were saying, "Jesus, tell us exactly and precisely **when** the temple will be destroyed, what is the sign of Your coming, and the sign indicating the end of the world." They felt the liberty to ask the Lord for very specific, concrete information, and so should you.

'WHAT shall be the SIGN of thy coming?' In this second question, we see the word "what," which is the little Greek word *ti*, and it describes *the most minute, minuscule detail.* This word is the equivalent of the disciples saying, "Lord, we don't want general information. We want You to tell us *exactly* and *explicitly — down to the most minute detail —* **what** will be the sign of Your coming?"

Then Jesus' most devoted followers asked Him for the *sign* of His coming, and this word "sign" in Matthew 24:3 is the Greek word *semeion*. It describes *a marker or sign to alert a traveler to where he is on a road.* An example would be the *road signs* you would find outside of Rick and Denise's home city of Moscow, as Rick described in the program.

As the Renners travel from their home in a suburb of Moscow toward the metropolis of Moscow, there are *signs* along the way to tell them where they are and how much farther they have to go. If there were no signs, they wouldn't know where they were on the journey. Various signs along the route inform them of the distance to their destination. When the Renners finally cross the Moscow Automobile Ring Road (MKAD), which is the circular road that runs predominantly around the border of the city, there's a huge sign that says "Moscow." Once they see that sign, they know they're no longer journeying *toward* Moscow, but they've entered Moscow itself.

This word "sign" — the Greek word *semeion* — is what the disciples asked for in Matthew 24:3, and it was the equivalent of saying, "Lord, what will be the specific *sign* we'll see along the prophetic road to tell us where we are in the journey — how far we've come and how much farther we have to go?"

'And of the END of the WORLD.' The third question the disciples asked Jesus was, "What is the sign of the *end* of the *world*." The Greek word for "end" here is the word *sunteleias*, and instead of describing absolute finality, it denotes the *closure* or *wrap-up of something*. This brings us to the word "world," which is the Greek word *aionos*, and rather than describe the world, the earth, or the universe, it describes *the present age*. Thus, a better translation of this portion of the verse would be, "How will we know that we're approaching the closure or the wrap-up of the present age?"

Jesus Warned Us of Great Deception

It's interesting to note that when people talk and teach about the signs of the end times, they often jump straight to verses 6 and 7 of Matthew 24, which forewarns of wars and rumors of wars, earthquakes, famines, and nation rising against nation, yet that is not the sign Jesus first mentioned. The Bible says, "And Jesus answered and said unto them, Take heed that no man deceive you" (Matthew 24:4). Here we understand the first sign we can expect to see before Jesus comes and this present age wraps up: worldwide *deception*.

The phrase "take heed" is the Greek word *blepete*, a form of the word *blepo*, which in this verse means *to watch*, *listen*, and *pay attention*. Here, Jesus was speaking in very strong terms to jar and jolt His listeners. It's as if He was saying, "Stand up, throw your shoulders back, open your ears, listen, be attentive, and pay attention."

Once Jesus grabbed hold of His disciples with His words, He unveiled the first and foremost sign that will mark the end of the age. He said, "…Take heed that no man deceive you" (Mathew 24:4). The word "deceive" here is a translation of the Greek word *planao*, which means *to lead astray*, and it describes *one who errs from a path that he has regularly walked upon*. In fact, it is the picture of *a person who has habitually walked upon a well-worn path*. It is the path on which he has always lived, but now, for some reason, *he has veered from that path, and he has taken another route*.

The word "deceive" used in Matthew 24:4 can also mean *to wander off course*. It can depict *an individual who has wandered off course* or *a whole nation* or even *vast numbers of nations that have veered off course from a moral position they once held to be true*. The use of this word suggests *a moral wandering on a worldwide scale* at the close of the age.

Interestingly, the apostle Paul also used this word *planao* in several of his New Testament letters, including the second one he wrote to the Thessalonians. When he described the corrupt, end-time generation that would receive the Antichrist, he said, "And for this cause God shall send them strong delusion, that they should believe a lie" (2 Thessalonians 2:11). The word "delusion" in this verse is the Greek word *planao*.

Therefore, we could translate Jesus' words in Matthew 24:4 to say, "Listen up and pay close attention! If you want to know what the sign will be that you've come to the end of the age, here it is — *delusional spirits* will be released in the earth that will cause people to wander away from the proven path of morality and truth they once walked on. Be on guard against deception."

Friend, we're living in that day of delusion about which Jesus spoke. Even the intertestamental prophets and rabbis, who really focused on the end times, prophesied that at the very end of the age — before the coming of the Messiah — there would be a release of spirits into the earth that would cause people to believe delusionary things. This confirms the first and most prominent sign of *deception* that Jesus gave.

Paul Prophesied a 'Departure' From the Faith in the Last Days

The end of the age is also described in First Timothy 4:1, where Paul wrote, "Now the Spirit speaketh expressly, that in the latter times some shall depart from the faith, giving heed to seducing spirits, and doctrines of devils." The word "expressly" here is the Greek word *rhetos*, which is from the word *rhema*, and it means *concretely, emphatically, categorically*, or *beyond a shadow of doubt*.

So when Paul said, "Now the Spirit speaks *expressly*," he affirmed, "The Spirit speaks *categorically*..." or, "The Spirit speaks *unmistakably*..." or, "The Spirit speaks *emphatically*...." In other words, Paul was not describing something that *might* happen. He was talking about something that absolutely, positively, without question *will* take place, and he said it will occur "in the latter times."

In Greek, the word "latter" is the word *husteros*, which describes *the very end of something*. The word "times" in Greek is *kairos*, which is the word for *a season* or *specific age*. In the nautical world, the word for "latter" was used to describe *the very last port one stopped at on a voyage*. By using this word, Paul was saying, "When you've sailed to the very end of the age and there's no time left, some shall depart from the faith, giving heed to seducing spirits and doctrines of devils."

Notice that Paul did not say that people will *outrightly reject* the faith. He said, "...Some *shall depart from* the faith..." (1 Timothy 4:1). This phrase "shall depart from" is the Greek word *aphistemi*, which describes *a very slow, methodical transitioning away from what one once stood by and believed*. It is a picture of people gradually letting go of what they were believing and reaching over and embracing a new belief.

Isn't that amazing! The Holy Spirit prophetically pointed His finger more than 2,000 years into the future and said, "*Emphatically, categorically, and with certainty*, at the very end of the age, people will begin to put distance between themselves and what they once believed. They'll slowly step away from the solid, concrete teaching of Scripture — gradually and methodically transitioning one step at a time away from what they once wholeheartedly embraced and believed."

This agrees with what Jesus said in Matthew 24:4: "…Take heed that no man deceive you." In other words, "A day is coming at the very end of the age when people will begin to veer off course and morally wander from the time-tested path of truth." Indeed, we're living in that prophesied period, when people are questioning their morals and distancing themselves from the biblical standards they once embraced.

'Seducing Spirits and Doctrines of Demons'

What will cause people to deviate and wander away from godly principles? First Timothy 4:1 says they will give heed to "…seducing spirits, and doctrines of demons." The word "seducing" is again the Greek word *planao* — which is *a gradual moving away from the long-affirmed laws of Scripture*. This divergence from truth — a moral wandering — will be the work of *evil, unclean spirits that will cause people to be lured off track.*

Along with the efforts of evil, unclean spirits are what the Bible describes as "doctrines of devils." The word "doctrines" is the Greek word *didaskalia*, which describes *doctrine* and *teaching* but can also denote *well-packaged information*. The use of this word lets us know that at the very end of the age, the devil is not going to come with a pitchfork in his hand and horns on his head. He's going to come in the intellectual name of science and the sophisticated fanfare of Hollywood entertainment. His seductive voice will present *well-packaged information* that will cause people to abandon reason and veer into *unimaginable* moral decadence.

And notice it says these are doctrines of *devils*. The word "devils" in Greek is the word *daimonion*, which is the word for *demons* or *devils*. The ancient world believed this word described *spirits that cause delusion and insanity*. Therefore, those who embrace this well-packaged, devil-concocted misinformation will end up coming to crazy and chaotic conclusions.

Paul Described a Domino Effect of Degradation in His Letter to the Believers in Rome

Writing under the inspiration of the Holy Spirit, the apostle Paul provided us with several snapshots of what society will look like at the end of the age. We see this throughout his letters, including the book of Romans. In chapter 1, he wrote, "For the wrath of God is revealed from heaven against all ungodliness and unrighteousness of men, who hold the truth in unrighteousness" (Romans 1:18).

Certain people will suppress the truth. When Paul talks about men "who hold the truth in unrighteousness," the word "hold" would be better translated *to suppress*. These individuals have *heard* and *know* the truth, but *they no longer like the truth*, and therefore, they have decided to do all they can to *cancel* it. With every opportunity they get, they restrain, suppress, and put a lid on it. So it's not that they're ignorant of the truth — they're just trying to *bury* it, because if they live in the light of the truth, they'll be accountable for it.

Paul went on to say, "Because that which may be known of God is manifest in them; for God hath shewed it unto them. For the invisible things of him from the creation of the world are clearly seen, being understood by the things that are made, even his eternal power and Godhead; so that they are without excuse: Because that, when they knew God, they glorified him not as God, neither were thankful; but became vain in their imaginations…" (Romans 1:19-21).

People in society will become flawed in their thinking. The word "knew" in Romans 1:21 describes a society that has a general knowledge of God and a reverential fear of Him, but at the end of the age, they will cease to glorify Him or be thankful to Him for the things He has done. Instead, they will become *vain* in their imaginations. The word "vain" here is the Greek word *mataios*, which describes *something that is completely wasted*. And the word "imaginations" is a form of the Greek word *logismos*, which is where we get the words *logical thinking*. In this case, their logic is going to become completely flawed and wasted (vain, useless).

Darkness will permeate everywhere. As a result of their flawed thinking, Romans 1:21 says, "…Their foolish heart was darkened." To grasp what is being said here, think about what the heart does. It pumps and pumps and pumps blood. Every part of your body has blood in it because the heart is pumping blood throughout your system.

Through Paul, the Holy Spirit is informing us that when we come to the wrap-up of the age, the heart of society will begin to pump out *darkness*. And just like the human heart pumps blood, the heart of society will continue to pump more and more darkness everywhere until darkness permeates the world.

People who claim to be the wisest of all will become fools. The Bible goes on to say, "Professing themselves to be wise, they became fools" (Romans 1:22). The word "professing" would be better translated as *asserting* or *alleging*. Thus, the heart of society will *allege* or *claim* to be *wise*. This word "wise" is a form of the Greek word *sophos*, which describes *those who believe they're a cut above the rest of society*. These are people who claim to be "progressive" leaders of a new kind of thinking and vow to move the world in a bold, new direction.

The Bible says these individuals who assert themselves as being mentally more brilliant than others become *fools*. The word "fools" is a translation of the Greek word *moraine*, which is where we get the word "moron." Thus, a literal translation of Romans 1:22 would be, "While they asserted themselves to be on the edge of a new kind of thinking — brilliant and a cut above everyone else — the truth is, they became morons in the way that they think."

They will exchange the glory of God for idols. The apostle Paul continued in Romans 1:23: "And [they] changed the glory of the uncorruptible God into an image made like to corruptible man, and to birds, and fourfooted beasts, and creeping things." The word "changed" here is the Greek word *allasso*, which would be better translated *to exchange*. Thus, these individuals who claimed to be so wise became morons and exchanged the glory of the incorruptible God for an image resembling corruptible man, birds, four-footed beasts, and creeping things.

This verse is one of the most ingenious verses in the entire New Testament. In this one succinct statement, the apostle Paul described the history of idolatry in reverse. For example, starting at the end of the verse, Paul wrote about "creeping things." If you study the history of idolatry in the world, you'll discover that the first thing people worshipped was creeping things like snakes and beetles. This is especially true during the time of Egypt's domination as a world power.

As time went by, people began to worship four-footed beasts like cats and cows, and by the time you get to the Roman Empire, people were worshiping birds. That's why there was an eagle as part of the insignia of the Roman Empire — they were worshiping birds. Hence, we see in this verse that man's thinking started with the worship of creeping things, ascended to worshiping four-footed beasts, and then moved even higher to worshiping birds. Finally, *at the end of the age*, Paul said *man will be the center of his own worship*, and man will worship *man*. We could call it humanism on steroids, which is what we are experiencing today.

What Is God's Response to Such Ungodliness?

Paul answered this question in Romans 1:24. He said, "Wherefore God also gave them up to uncleanness through the lusts of their own hearts, to dishonour their own bodies between themselves." Now, people who have a problem with God often take this verse and claim that God gave up on them, but a careful look at the original text reveals otherwise.

The words "gave up" are a translation of the Greek word *paradiomi*, which means *to permit, to allow,* or *to give into the hands of another*. It carries the idea of *delivering* or *surrendering custody*. Thus, we could translate Romans 1:24 to say, "Wherefore God *released and surrendered custody* of them to uncleanness through the lusts of their own hearts, to dishonor their own bodies between themselves."

The use of this word *paradiomi* — translated here as "gave up" — tells us that God will let us worship anything we want to worship. If a person is bound and determined to exchange the worship of God for the worship of man, God will *release* that person to do so. It's as if God is saying, "You want that? Go ahead and get it."

This brings us to the word "uncleanness," which is the Greek word *akatharsia*, a word that always refers to *sexual uncleanness*. It is *unbridled, reckless, and licentious living* that takes its participants even deeper into sin. Specifically, Paul said they begin "…to dishonour their own bodies between themselves" (Romans 1:24). A better translation here would be that they *displaced their bodies* or *put their bodies where bodies don't naturally belong*, and this wrong combination of bodies is dishonoring.

The truth is, *we are living in the day of dishonoring the human body*. Just think of all the things that so many people are doing — things they would have never done years ago. Generally speaking, society believes it's fine to do anything you want to do to your body. You can pierce it and tattoo it however and wherever you desire — you can even kill a developing baby inside his or her mother's womb. A growing number have even gone so far as to mutilate their own body parts and to push for the mutilation of the reproductive organs of young children. This is a vivid picture of dishonoring the human body created in the image of God. It's a major sign that society is coming to the end of the age. Is it any wonder Jesus said, "…Take heed that no man deceive you" (Matthew 24:4).

God Will Release People
To Do What They Want To Do

What else does the Bible say about society in the last of the last days? It says that the people will have "...changed the truth of God into a lie, and worshipped and served the creature more than the Creator, who is blessed for ever. Amen" (Romans 1:25). When we take our eyes off God, we often begin looking at ourselves, and when *you* become the center of your own universe, you begin to "play God" in your life. In that position, you can make yourself be whatever you want to be — even if it defies nature.

Paul said, "For this cause God *gave them up*..." (Romans 1:26). Again, a better translation of this would be, "For this cause, God *released and surrendered custody* of them...." What did He release them or deliver them up to do? Scripture says, "...Unto vile affections: for even their women did change the natural use into that which is against nature: And likewise also the men, leaving the natural use of the woman, burned in their lust one toward another; men with men working that which is unseemly, and receiving in themselves that recompence of their error which was meet" (Romans 1:26,27).

In the next verse, Paul revealed how these individuals were rewarded for their actions. Romans 1:28 says, "And even as they did not like to retain God in their knowledge, God gave them over to a reprobate mind, to do those things which are not convenient." This verse informs us that these were not people who were ignorant of the truth. They *knew* the truth but decided they no longer wanted to believe it. Although they had walked on a solid path of truth for a time, something has seduced them in another direction. Consequently, they have distanced themself from truth, saying, "We don't want that anymore. We've already been there and done that, and now we're following the super intelligentsia of society — the progressive thinkers that are leading us in a new direction."

Little by Little, We've Become
a 'Reprobate' Generation

The Bible says, "...God gave them over [released them] to a reprobate mind..." (Romans 1:28). In Greek, the word "reprobate" is *adokimos*, a combination of the word *dokimos* with an "*a*" attached to the front of it. The word *dokimos* describes *something that is wonderful, fit, and marvelous,* but when an "a" is placed on the front, it's *adokimos* — the word "reprobate." This describes *a person who was created by God with a wonderfully brilliant mind, but because his or her mind has been inundated repeatedly with wrong information, it has now become ill-affected.* Thus, a "reprobate" is *a mentally modified condition* in which a person's mind has been modified to think something different than what he or she used to believe.

Interestingly, Isaiah prophesied nearly 2,700 years ago that this would take place. He said, "Woe unto them that call evil good, and good evil; that put darkness for light, and light for darkness; that put bitter for sweet, and sweet for bitter!" (Isaiah 5:20) Right now — at the very end of the age — people are calling evil good and good evil. Likewise, they have exchanged light for darkness. In other words, things that were universally celebrated as life-giving and illuminating have been replaced with dark, evil practices. How can that be? It is because people have been so mentally modified that they no longer know what is light and what is darkness or what is good and what is bad. This is the process of mental modification, which the Bible translates as the word "reprobate."

Look around you. The earmarks of a reprobate generation are all around us. Right now there are people who claim to be the leaders of a new kind of progressive thinking who are targeting our children as young as age three, making them question if they're really the gender they were born with. This is the very definition of mental modification the Bible calls *reprobate.* These so-called elites of society are trying again and again and again to modify the thinking of our children with the goal of redefining evil as good and good as evil.

Many of today's universities and colleges are run by policies and filled with teachers who are trying to manipulate and change the way our young people think. Likewise, the media, fashion, and entertainment industries are all pushing for new levels of perversity and absolute wickedness to be celebrated as the norm. Indeed, we're living in an age of rebellion, anarchy, and lawlessness that is unprecedented. In fact, there is so much rebellion that we have reached the point when people are rebelling against their own gender. These are the very things Jesus and the apostle Paul prophesied would take place at the end of the age.

Deception and the 'Falling Away'

Jesus said, "…Take heed that no man deceive you" (Matthew 24:4). In other words, "Watch and listen! You'll know you've come to the end of the age when you see the sign of worldwide deception (*planao*). Delusional spirits will cause people to veer off the proven path of morality and truth they once walked on." The apostle Paul echoed this same warning of apostasy in First Timothy 4:1 when he said that the Holy Spirit emphatically declared that people would gradually distance themselves from the faith because they would be listening to "seducing spirits and doctrines of devils."

Again, the word "seducing" in First Timothy 4:1 and the word "deceive" in Matthew 24:4 is the same Greek word *planao*. It's interesting to note that this word *planao* could also be used to describe *a person that is walking and teetering right on the edge of a dangerous cliff*. Additionally, it was used by farmers to describe *an animal that had gotten so far off track, it could never find its way back home*. It is this same word — *planao* — that the Holy Spirit uses to describe the condition of society at the end of the age.

When the apostle Paul wrote to the believers in Thessalonica, it was to correct the wrong information they had received. Apparently, someone had told them that Jesus had already returned to rapture, or "catch away," the Church. Therefore, they believed they had been left behind. To comfort their hearts and minds and amend their thinking, Paul wrote and told them, "Let no man deceive you by any means: for that day shall not come, except there come a falling away first, and that man of sin be revealed, the son of perdition" (2 Thessalonians 2:3).

When Paul referred to "that day," it was regarding the day Jesus returns to catch the Church away in the clouds. He said *that day* will not happen until the *falling way* occurs first. The words "falling away" are a translation of the Greek word *apostasia*, which is where we get the word "apostasy." It is the very word used all over the Septuagint to describe *a mutinous attitude*. Here in Second Thessalonians 2:3, the apostle Paul prophesied that at the end of the age, there will be *a mutinous attitude against God*, *against the Word of God*, and *against God's laws and standards*.

Once this "falling away" (*apostasia*) takes place, "…that man of sin [will] be revealed, the son of perdition" (2 Thessalonians 2:3). The phrase "man of sin" in Greek is the word *anomia*. It is a form of the word *nomos*, which is the Greek word for *law*, but with an "*a*" on the front of it. When it becomes *anomia*, it describes *one that has cast off all shackles, all moral restraints, and all the law of God.* Here we see that at the end of the age, when society develops a mutinous attitude (*apostasia*), the world itself will produce a man of their own making — *the man of lawlessness* who is also known as the *Antichrist*.

What Is Stopping the Advancement of Evil?

When we come to Second Thessalonians 2:6, Paul began to describe what is stopping the advancement of evil. He says, "And now ye know what withholdeth that he might be revealed in his time" (2 Thessalonians 2:6). The word "withholdeth" is the Greek word *katecho*, which means *to hold fast; to hold down; to hold back; to suppress; to restrain*, or *to hinder*. A better translation of this verse would be, "Now you know what is *restraining, suppressing, stalling, and holding back* all the floodgates of evil from pouring into and taking over the world that he [the Antichrist] might be revealed in his time."

Paul went on to say, "For the mystery of iniquity doth already work: only he who now letteth will let, until he be taken out of the way" (2 Thessalonians 2:7). The word "mystery" is the Greek word *musterion*, and it describes *a mystery* or *secret; something once hidden, but now revealed*. This word carries the idea of a secret plan that has been hidden from the masses and only a select few are aware of it.

Paul said it is the mystery of "iniquity," and the Greek word for "iniquity" is *anomia* — the same word translated as "sin" in Second Thessalonians 2:3. It means *lawlessness, without law*, or *a lawless attitude*. Thus, the "mystery of iniquity" would be better translated *the secret plan of lawlessness*. This dark, hidden agenda of the enemy is not a new development but has been at "work" for quite some time, which literally means *a force has been propelling lawlessness forward and facilitating its full development.*

The mystery of iniquity will continue to grow in strength and expand its influence "...until he [the restrainer] be taken out of the way" (*see* 2 Thessalonians 2:7). The word "until" is the Greek word *heos*, and it means *until that precise moment*. The phrase "be taken" in Greek is *genetai*, which is from the word *ginomai*, and it describes *a surprising event — something that happens suddenly or unexpectedly and totally takes one off guard.*

The Restrainer is us — the Church. In a sudden, surprising move, "he" — the Restrainer — will be snatched out of the way and into Heaven. This is a description of the Rapture, which will take place in a moment, in the twinkling of an eye. Suddenly, in a split second, the dead in Christ will come back to life, and the remnant of believers alive on the earth — the Restrainer — will be snatched up. The Bible says we will be taken "out of the way." This phrase is a translation of the Greek words *ek mesou*. It means *out of the middle; out of the midst; out of the middle of things*.

What would happen in the world today if, suddenly, every Christ follower was evacuated? There would be nothing left to stall, postpone, or put the brakes on evil. Once we are suddenly removed from the midst of every-thing, the Bible says, "…Then shall that Wicked be revealed, whom the Lord shall consume with the spirit of his mouth, and shall destroy with the brightness of his coming" (2 Thessalonians 2:8).

This verse tells us clearly that the moment the Church is evacuated, the curtains are going to part, and "that Wicked [will] be revealed." In Greek, the words "that Wicked" is *ho anomos*, meaning *the Wicked One* or *the Lawless One*. In other words, this is not just your average evil person; he is the epitome of wickedness himself, and he will take center stage once the Church is evacuated.

As long as we — the Church — are here, we have the power of the Holy Spirit within us to hold back evil. Even though we don't always do everything we should do, and we don't always do things right, the fact is, God is in the Church, and He is holding back and restraining Satan's full takeover of the world through us. The Antichrist cannot be revealed and take centerstage until the Church has been removed.

In the Last Days, We Will Experience 'Perilous Times'

When we go to Second Timothy 3:1, we get yet another glimpse of what the world will be like just before the return of Christ. Paul said, "This know also, that in the last days perilous times shall come." In this verse, there are several key words, including the first word "this." It is the Greek word *touto*, and it emphatically points to a very specific thing. Basically, Paul said, "Categorically, know this thing…."

The word "know" here is a form of the Greek word *ginosko*, which means *to personally and intimately know, understand, and perceive something*. By saying, "This know also," it's as if Paul is reaching through the pages in order to grab us and get our attention. Then he adds the word "that" — the Greek word *hoti* — which is a "pointer word" that is pointing at a very important conclusion. Paul said, "...In the last days perilous times shall come" (2 Timothy 3:1).

The word "last" is the Greek word *eschatos*, which is where we get the term "eschatology," *the study of end times*. This word *eschatos* always describes *the very end of a thing*. For example, *eschatos* would describe *the last day of the week*, *the last day of the month*, or *the last month of the year*. In the New Testament, it was used to describe *the very ends of the earth*.

It was also used in a navigational sense to describe *a ship that has sailed to the last port*. Once that ship has reached its final stop (*eschatos*), there are no other ports after it. This last port signifies the end of the journey. By using the word *eschatos*, Paul was literally saying, "You really need to know and understand that when we have sailed to the very last port in time and there's no more time left on the journey, perilous times shall come."

Perilous times are treacherous times. This brings us to the word "perilous," which is the Greek word *chalepos*, a word that is only used two times in the New Testament. To understand its meaning here, let's look at its use in Matthew 8:28, which says, "And when he [Jesus] was come to the other side into the country of the Gergesenes, there met him two possessed with devils, coming out of the tombs, *exceeding fierce*, so that no man might pass by that way."

Notice the words "exceeding fierce." They are a translation of the word *chalepos*, which describes *something so dangerous that it should be avoided at all costs — something so treacherous, if you get near it, there's a possibility of great personal injury*. The Bible states these two devil-possessed men were so exceedingly fierce that "...no man might pass by that way" (Matthew 8:28).

It's important to note that in First Century Israel, there was a highway that went around the perimeter of the Sea of Galilee. If you were in the north of Galilee and you wanted to go south, you would travel on the east side, which would put you on the very road where you would have to pass by these two demon-possessed men. The Bible says they were "exceedingly fierce" (*chalepos*). Thus, they posed a high risk and a great threat to everyone who passed by.

History tells us that when people tried to pass on that road to the south of Galilee, these demon-possessed men would come charging out of the tombs and wreak havoc on them. They were so hazardous that people were afraid to take that route. Hence, the presence of the demon-possessed men formed *an impasse* or *blockade*. All this meaning is found in the word "perilous," the Greek word *chalepos*.

When we take this meaning in Greek and insert it into Second Timothy 3:1, we could translate it to read, "Emphatically know and understand this — that when time has sailed to its last port and no time is left on the journey, society as a whole will feel it has entered a hazardous period of great danger — an impasse in society that people will not know how to get around."

We're surrounded by craziness. Second Timothy 3:1 ends with the word "shall come," which is a translation of the Greek word *enistemi*, a compound of the words *en* and *histemi*. The preposition *en* means *to be in the middle of something*, and the word *histemi* describes *something that's standing all around you*. When these words are compounded to form *enistemi* — translated here as "shall come," it describes *a person in the middle of something*, and wherever he turns — everywhere that individual looks — he's surrounded or encumbered by that thing.

Thus, through Paul, the Holy Spirit is telling us that at the very end of the age, people in society will feel as though they've hit an impasse in the world, and everywhere they turn, things will appear to be dangerously hazardous and crazy. Does that sound familiar? Have you seen anything like this? Everywhere we look, it's like we're living in the age of craziness. This is a major confirmation that we have arrived at the end of the age. The Holy Spirit is not telling us these things to scare us but to prepare us for things to come.

What's the Solution
To Living in Deceptive, Crazy Times?

After Paul described a laundry list of end-time attitudes and activities in society, he stated, "But evil men and seducers shall wax worse and worse, deceiving, and being deceived" (2 Timothy 3:13). The word "wax" here is the Greek word *prokopto*, which means *to increase, advance,* or *make progress*. Interestingly, it is the very word that was used to describe *the advancement of gangrene* or *the advancement of cancer*. The use of this word *prokopto* indicates that this delusional and deceptive teaching is going to try to work its way throughout the fabric of society in order to infect it.

To effectively deal with this dilemma, Paul said, "But continue thou in the things which thou hast learned and hast been assured of, knowing of whom thou hast learned them" (2 Timothy 3:14). The word "continue" is a translation of the Greek word *meno*, which means *to stay in your place and refuse to flinch or budge.* It's the same word that means *to maintain the territory you have gained.* In other words, even if it seems that the world around us is losing its mind, we need to keep our head on straight.

Paul urged Timothy — and *us* — to *continue* in the things we've learned and been assured of, knowing from whom we've learned them. He continued, "…From a child you have known the holy *scriptures*, which are able to make thee wise unto salvation through faith which is in Christ Jesus" (2 Timothy 3:15).

Here, Paul elevates the "Scriptures," which is the Greek word *gramma*. It describes not just a verse or a book but *the entirety of God's Word* and includes every little mark, every little jot, and every little tittle. It's as if Paul said, "Every dotted 'i,' every crossed 't,' every comma, and every period in the Bible is sacred and extremely valuable." If we continue in the Scriptures and embrace them, Paul said, "…[They're] able to make thee wise unto salvation through faith which is in Christ Jesus" (2 Timothy 3:15).

The word "able" here is the Greek word *dunatos*, a form of the word *dunamai*, which means *to be able or capable* or *have power and ability of doing something.* In this case, the Scriptures have the power to make us *wise.* This word "wise" is a form of the Greek word *sophos*, which here means *to make wise* or *to have understanding.* The use of *sophos* in this verse tells us that if we want to be smart, we need to stick with the Bible because the Bible will fill our mind with enlightenment and give us common sense. Without question, chewing on the meat of God's Word enables our senses to be "…exercised to discern both good and evil" (Hebrews 5:14).

Is it any wonder the devil has been trying to purge the Bible from our churches? Sadly, a vast number of churches today don't hear verse-by-verse teaching of Scripture, which is why so many people are confused. Although there's a great deal of inspirational teaching, which definitely has its place, the verse-by-verse teaching of Scripture provides answers to every question that arises — in Scripture and in life. When you deal with each verse in the context of the Bible itself, it sobers you up so you can think *wisely*.

All Scripture Is 'Given by Inspiration of God'

When we come to Second Timothy 3:16, we discover one of the most important verses in the Bible. Here Paul explained, "All scripture is given by inspiration of God, and is profitable for doctrine, for reproof, for correction, for instruction in righteousness." Notice the phrase "given by inspiration of God." This is a translation of the Greek word *theopneustos*, which is a compound of the word *theo* and *pneustos*. The word *theo* comes from *theos* and is where we get the word "*theology*," the Greek word for "God." The second part of *theopneustos* is the word *pneustos*, which comes from the word *pneo* and has three primary meanings, all of which are correct in this verse.

#1: Creative Power. The word *pneo*, the second part of the word "inspiration," was used to describe *creative power*. This is the word that appears in the account of creation in Genesis 1 of the Greek Septuagint. The Bible says, "In the beginning God created the heaven and the earth. And the earth was without form, and void; and darkness was upon the face of the deep. And the Spirit of God moved upon the face of the waters" (Genesis 1:1,2). When God came, He released *creative power* to make order out of chaos and darkness. That power is the word *pneo*.

#2: Beautiful Music. The word *pneo* was also the Greek word used to describe *the sounds of music*. If you put a flute to your mouth and begin to blow into the flute, alternating your fingers to cover certain holes, your breath can create *beautiful music*.

#3: A Perfume or Fragrance. The word *pneo* was also used by Greeks and Romans to describe *perfume* or *a fragrance*. If you went into a store to buy a new fragrance or perfume, you would have gone in and said, "I'd like to buy some *pneo*."

So when Paul said in Second Timothy 3:16, "All Scripture is given by inspiration of God," he was telling us that all Scripture has *creative power*, produces *beautiful music*, and exudes a sweet *perfume* or *fragrance*.

Keep in mind that for the entire chapter of Second Timothy 3, Paul talked about the last-days society that has gone crazy. The people are self-focused, self-absorbed narcissists that are extremely messed up. What's the proven cure for the chaotic craziness plaguing society? *It is the Word of God!*

All Scripture is God-breathed and has *creative power* (*pneo*). It is especially gifted to create order out of chaos and darkness. If you have darkness in your life, embrace God's Word and let it work in you. It will bring order into your life again.

All Scripture is God-breathed and produces *beautiful music* (*pneo*). If you don't like the sound of what is going on in your life, bring the Word of God into it. If you'll begin to meditate on and speak the Word, your mind will be renewed, and the sounds of Heaven will be released into your home and into the atmosphere of your life.

All Scripture is God-breathed and emits a *perfume or fragrance* (*pneo*). If you don't like the "stink" that's going on in your life, your family, your finances, or your friendships, bring the Word of God into them, because the Word is God-breathed. If you'll hold tightly to and begin speaking God's Word, it will release a sweet-smelling fragrance into your life.

God's Word Will Put You Back on Your Feet and Fully Equip You To Fulfill Your Calling

After Paul declared that "All scripture is given by inspiration of God…," he then added, "…And is profitable for doctrine, for reproof, for correction, for instruction in righteousness" (2 Timothy 3:16). The word "correction" here is the Greek term *epanorthosis*, which describes *a person that has been knocked flat by life but has been picked up and put back on their feet again.* Have you or someone you know been knocked flat by life? Believing and embracing the Word of God is vital to your recovery. It has the power to pick you up and put you on your feet again — regardless of what has happened to you or how "messed up" your life has become!

The ultimate goal of the Word of God is "that the man of God may be perfect, thoroughly furnished unto all good works" (*see* 2 Timothy 3:17). The key phrase to pay attention to in this verse is "thoroughly furnished." It is a translation of the old Greek word *exartidzo*, which was only used one way: to describe *something that is fully equipped.*

Back in the ancient world, several types of boats were used for transportation and for moving goods from one location to another. Among them was a very simple boat that was used by many. In fact, it appears that the boat manufacturers on the Sea of Galilee must have had a monopoly over the boating industry because virtually everyone who sailed the Sea of Galilee used the same model of boat. Unfortunately, it couldn't go very far because it wasn't designed for long-term sailing or for handling the high seas during rough weather. Consequently, it always seemed to be heading back to shore.

What's interesting is that you could take the very same boat and *thoroughly furnish* it, and it would become equipped to do what it couldn't do before. For instance, if you added oars, a sail, a motor, and other needed equipment to a simple boat today, that same simple boat would become transformed into a vessel that could weather raging storms, plow through turbulent seas, and handle long-distance sailing — all because it has been *thoroughly furnished.*

Paul used this analogy of being "thoroughly furnished" (*exartidzo*) to teach us that all Christians are like boats, and we each fall into one of two categories: *the unequipped Christian* and *the equipped Christian.* Believers who lack understanding of and obedience to God's Word are not equipped for long distances — neither can they make it through tough times. In contrast, believers who take the Word of God into their lives and put it into practice are thoroughly furnished with the spiritual equipment needed to weather life's storms and go the distance. It's as if the Scriptures outfit you with spiritual oars, a sail, a strong rudder, and a motor so you can get where you need to go and accomplish your God-given destiny!

The Essential Meaning of Second Timothy 3:1 and 17

Writing under the inspiration of the Holy Spirit, Paul masterfully used this nautical theme throughout the entire third chapter of Second Timothy. Again, when we insert the original Greek meaning into Second Timothy 3:1, it could be translated, *"Emphatically know and understand this — that when you've sailed to the very last port and no time is left on the journey, society as a whole will feel as if it has entered a hazardous period of great danger. Extremely rough and turbulent conditions in society will seem to be impossible to navigate around."*

Thankfully, God doesn't leave us with this bleak and dismal forecast. Through Paul, He reminds us of the vital importance and power of His Word and how it equips us with everything we need. When we insert the original Greek into Second Timothy 3:17, it could be translated, *"God has given you everything you need in His Word to be fully equipped to sail through the darkest and most turbulent of times. Scripture thoroughly furnishes you to do good works and go the distance all the way to the other side."*

Stick With the Word!

Friend, we're living in a world that is trapped in deep darkness. Many people's lives are totally messed up and broken, and nothing about their story sounds good. They're angry, depressed, and even suicidal because of the foul-smelling situations they're living in. If this describes you, it's time to grab hold of the Word of God and begin to regularly take it in! It has everything you need to release creative power, bring the music of Heaven into any situation, and generate a sweet new smell in your marriage, your family, and your life.

If people all around you seem to be drifting away from God and embracing the corrupt thinking of this world, don't let it move you. Stay the course and stay in the Scriptures. And if your children seem to be departing (*aphistemi*) from the faith because of the misguided influence of their friends, their teachers, and the ungodly entertainment industry, pray for them and don't compromise on the Word. If you back away from what you know to be true in Scripture and go along with the ungodly choices others around you are making, everyone will suffer in the end.

Remember God's promise: "Train up a child in the way he should go: and when he is old, he will not depart from it" (Proverbs 22:6). The day will come when your children may be in trouble, and if you haven't caved in and gone along with their ungodly choices, they will eventually turn to you for help and answers to the problems they're facing. The Word of God is the answer for all of us in these troubling times, so stick with the Word!

Here's a prayer you can pray from your heart to invite the presence and power of God into your life:

> *Father, thank You for giving me Your amazing Word! Please help me to regularly feed on its truths and put it into practice in my life. Help me to remember to proclaim it in my prayers, declare it against the devil, and speak it over myself and my family. May my children and grandchildren personally discover the power of Your Word and develop the healthy habit of feeding their spirits with it every day. Let Your*

truth not return void in all our lives. I call forth a harvest of rich,
eternal fruit. In Jesus' mighty name. Amen.

STUDY QUESTIONS

Study to shew thyself approved unto God, a workman that
needeth not to be ashamed, rightly dividing the word of truth.
— 2 Timothy 2:15

1. In this teaching, we learned about the connection between "deception and the falling away" and "what is stopping the advancement of evil." Carefully reread these sections along with Second Thessalonians 2:1-8. What do these verses and excerpts show you about the sequence of events concerning the Rapture, the rapid spread of evil, the falling away, and the coming of the Antichrist on the world scene? What is the biblical order in which they take place and why is it important?

2. The rapture of the Church is the most exciting and most anticipated event for believers who long to be forever with Jesus! According to First Corinthians 15:51-53 and First Thessalonians 4:15-18, what can you expect to take place when we — the Church — are raptured by Jesus? What connection can you see between these passages and Jesus' words in John 14:2,3? What else does the Bible specifically say about the Rapture and Jesus' appearing in Matthew 24:36-42; Luke 17:34,35; Philippians 3:20,21; Colossians 3:4; and First John 3:2?

3. To successfully navigate the raging storms of these last days, we need the equipping of the Word of God. What will embracing God's Word do in *your* life? Check out these promises and write out the positive impact you can expect to experience from feeding on the Word!

   • 1 Peter 2:2; Psalm 119:103; Jeremiah 15:16

   • John 8:31,32

   • Acts 20:32

   • Hebrews 4:12

   • Ephesians 5:26,27 and John 17:17

   • James 1:21-25

4. As you regularly hide God's Word in your heart (*see* Psalm 119:11), your mind will be renewed with truth (*see* Romans 12:2), and the

sword of the Spirit will be ready in your hand (*see* Ephesians 6:17). In what specific areas is the enemy fighting hard against you? Is it thoughts of sexual impurity? Worry about finances? Fear of the future? Using an online Bible search engine or a Bible concordance, begin looking up key words related to what you're facing. As you find scriptures that demolish the devil's lies and bring you hope and encouragement, write them down and begin to *speak them* over your life and against the enemy. Then watch in amazement at how the weapon of God's Word brings breakthrough! (*See* Jesus' example in Luke 4:1-4.)

PRACTICAL APPLICATION

But be ye doers of the word, and not hearers only,
deceiving your own selves.
—James 1:22

1. Since Jesus Himself said deception would be at an all-time high just before He returns, it is vital that we guard our heart and mind against deception. Take a moment and pray, *Lord, is there an area in my life where I'm deceived? Where am I believing a lie — about You, about myself, or about something else? Please show me what I cannot see and lead me to the truth. In Jesus' name.*

2. God spoke through Isaiah and said, "Woe unto them that call evil good, and good evil…" (Isaiah 5:20). In what specific ways are you seeing this prophecy being fulfilled in society today? How are people calling evil good and good evil?

3. The Bible says that at the very end of the age, "…some shall depart from the faith…" (1 Timothy 4:1). Do you know someone who seems to be slowly and methodically moving away from his or her faith in Christ and the truth of the Bible that person once stood by and believed? What "new beliefs" is that individual embracing? What can you learn from that person's choices to keep you from departing from *your* own faith in Christ?

4. Paul used the nautical analogy of a boat being "thoroughly furnished" (*exartidzo*) to teach us that all Christians fall into one of two categories: we are either an *equipped* Christian or an *unequipped* Christian. Be honest: Which one would you consider yourself to be? What

category do you think your closest friends would put you in? What evidence backs up your answer?

5. To avoid the deadly trap of deception, you need to know the truth of God's Word. Indeed, the Holy Scriptures "…are able to make thee wise unto salvation through faith which is in Christ Jesus" (2 Timothy 3:15). On a scale of 1 to 10 (1 being terrible, 10 being terrific), how would you rate your personal time in God's Word? What can you delete from your daily schedule to make room for reading and studying Scripture? Pray and ask the Holy Spirit for His creative wisdom.

---

[1] *Webster's Dictionary 1828*, s.v. "deceive," https://webstersdictionary1828.com

[2] Josephus, *Antiquities of the Jews*, XV, 11.3; *Jewish Wars*, V. 5.

Notes

Notes

_____

_____

_____

_____

_____

_____

_____

_____

_____

_____

_____

_____

_____

_____

_____

_____

_____

_____

_____

_____

_____

_____

_____

_____

_____

_____

_____

CLAIM YOUR FREE RESOURCE!

As a way of introducing you further to the teaching ministry of Rick Renner, we would like to send you FREE of charge his teaching, "How To Receive a Miraculous Touch From God" on CD or USB format.

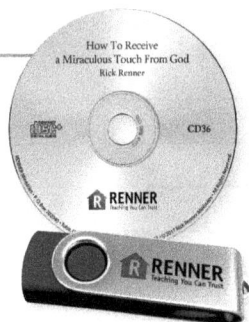

In His earthly ministry, Jesus commonly healed *all* who were sick of *all* their diseases. In this profound message, learn about the manifold dimensions of Christ's wisdom, goodness, power, and love toward all humanity who came to Him in faith with their needs.

☑ **YES, I want to receive Rick Renner's monthly teaching letter!**

Simply scan the QR code to claim this resource or go to:
renner.org/claim-your-free-offer

Connect

WITH US!